DEWY BROWN EYES: HEAL

Wilfredo B. de Leon

Willys Publishing
A division of Willys LLC
Phoenix, Arizona

This is a work of creative non-fiction. The poems reflect the author's lived experiences and inner truths, interwoven with creative interpretation.

ISBN 978-1-23456-789-0 (Paperback)

Illustrations by Wilfredo B. de Leon with assistance from AI tools

Published by Willys Publishing
Philadelphia, Pennsylvania

Printed in the United States of America

willys
PUBLISHING

With gratitude to all
who contributed their
time and support to
bring this vision to life.

Table of Content

Introduction

Years ago I decided to take ownership of my healing by acknowledging that the only way to grow into the person I dreamt of becoming was to address anything holding me back from obtaining it.

What started as scattered journal entries, became a ritual: write, reflect, breathe, heal. I revisited moments that shaped me, fractured me, and eventually, rebuilt me. Through meditation, stillness, and therapy, I began to face what once silenced me.

If you're carrying something too heavy to speak aloud, I hope these pages remind you that you're not alone. That healing is messy and holy. That we all deserve the chance to fly, even with broken wings.

Let's soar, together.

- **Wilfredo**

Reality

A mosaic of expectations,
shaped the rigid molds of men,
stealing the chance to become
in the early seasons of youth

Drifting through the past,
searching for a way back home,
I find my reflection carved
with scars of insecurity

The pieces of me they feared
became the vessel of their disdain,
a burden I carried
that was never mine

My first taste of reality

Frustration

Frustration pulled me inward
through the corridors of the mind
whispers in fragments
breath drawn from shadows

Wandering the halls
searching for a quiet flame,
a pulse beneath the silence

There,
in a realm of solace
I uncovered the essence
of my fundamental self

Wanting

The reality is
I have clawed at doors
that would not open,

whispered to walls
that would not listen,

and still I stay
aching for a crack of light

The
weight
of
wanting
to
be
"normal"

but even locked doors
are not the end

sometimes,
the lesson is not in the opening
but in learning where to knock

Youth

In the midst of self-discovery
suppressed by a world
unwilling to embrace
the spectrum of love
stretching beyond
conventional boundaries

A multitude of influences
interwove to sculpt my identity,
a delicate dance,
conformity and expression
waltz to the tune of chaos

Concealing the vibrant colors of individuality
I fled inward for comfort
But the lies I told others
were the lies I told myself
forming a web of deception
separating me
from the youthful boy that once was

Silence

There are times
when silence
is a heavy thing
settling dust on the words
never spoken

In a queue
waiting
patiently
waiting

Silence has a way of shifting
turning from weight to wind
carrying us
before we even realize
we are moving forward

Unconscious

In the realm of hidden depths
we dwell
where thoughts and dreams
unknowingly swell

Memories tucked away
our souls are free to wander
to seek what thoughts ignored
secrets whisper
the unconscious mind
there it lies

In a symphony of colors
dancing like fireflies
in the night
guided by the moon's
mystical light
shadows deep
a dream formed
that made me weep

Unconscious,
the resting place of the soul
the boundless space within
the canvas of the mind
hidden treasures
we often find
as it wanders
through the pulses
of the cosmic mind

Embrace this realm unseen
where wonders convene
and let us delve into the
depths unknown
for there lies the beauty
yet to be shown

Time sailed
yet do not remember
for we were
in the world within

World Within

In the sanctuary of a curated world
the mind evolved into a refuge
where self-expression flowed

Essence,
a directionless energy
wandering through a distant dream,
the world within

Perched upon the throne of my kingdom,
embarking on a journey
guided by the compass of aspiration,
the manifestation formed

All that I aspired to be
lies within the world of my creation
And to obtain it,
I must venture into the unknown

Unknown

I went down to the river
to find a stream of opportunities
A strong sense of desire
to reconnect with reality arose

The vision was manifesting
but the weight of the words
they said to me
that I said to myself
anchored in a hideaway carved by pain
my inner world

Years were sacrificed
remained lost because growth was unsettling
Stuck in a loop of habits
reducing myself to fit in
I wore myself out
lugging around armor

Screaming out to the universe for
health, wealth, happiness
beauty, grace, wisdom
to breathe without suffering
for consciousness in life

I stripped down and walked into the river
still for a moment
while the current
pushed against the fear
I took a deep breath and dove in

Drifting down the stream
flowing naturally through life
I looked up at the sky and saw a reflection

To be free I needed to let go
to heal I needed to be reborn
Wash away the layers
to find a boy searching for self

Feeling that I could
reconnect with reality
a spark of hope brewed
to keep flowing on

Letting gravity ground
mind and body
this journey is uncertain
but the vision is clear
I was taken into the unknown
and allowed life to flow freely

Resilience

I almost drowned
beneath the tide
but even the ocean
knows how to carry
what refuses to sink
it makes you think
resilience is not only
to stand against the waves
but to flow with them
to breathe in their rhythm

Imagination

Imagination
the spark that saved tomorrow
a whisper of being
when being felt impossible
without it
words would halt
breath would break
pain would stand still
yet a colorful mind
born of darkness
gave the days a chance

Lost

Some things grow

without being seen

they surface beneath the frost,

in half-light they bloom

at first breath, they gleam

manifestations into blessings unseen

The journey through life

can feel like a dream,

but one thing is certain:

not everything forgotten

is lost

Truth

Speechless, our minds restless,
an internal fight
between the worlds we occupy
We sit in silence, processing pain,
waiting for words to heal us

In quiet introspection,
the mind is a battlefield
longing to be mastered
Each breath unraveling
our delicate truth

And in the hands of a healer
a promised light
to spaces that birth
the chance to unfold
the intricate layers
that shape us

Formation

Change does not come in storms
it arrives gently

Truth does not arrive with a shout
it comes in the quiet
in the spaces between breaths
during the stillness that once felt empty

With each syllable spoken
we begin to recognize
the shape of who we are becoming

Becoming

Floating aimlessly in time
the youth I once was
became a lighthouse
to navigate back to the core of my being

Ushered towards rediscovery
fragments of self
were gathered along the way
encountering the resilience
that sustained me through the years

Those dewy brown eyes
once dimmed with shame
radiated vibrantly
with each revelation:

Stillness ignites bursts of introspection
Authenticity is paramount
Becoming is a lifelong journey

Home

Spent a lifetime chasing
leaving and returning
to the same place
a desperate grasp
for something
just beyond reach
and yet,
I remain in myself
and see the truth
I was never lost
nor incomplete
every version remains
only now,
I call it home

Within all of us
there is a core being
waiting to be discovered
free from ego and suffering

Aura
a fuel to reclaim ourselves
when we forget
that we have been within all along

thank you for your joy, imagination and strength